The Sky's Larger Frame

The Sky's Larger Frame

Randall Compton

RESOURCE *Publications* · Eugene, Oregon

THE SKY'S LARGER FRAME

Resource Publications
An Imprint of Wipf and Stock Publishers
199 W. 8th Ave., Suite 3
Eugene, OR 97401

www.wipfandstock.com

PAPERBACK ISBN: 978-1-5326-8231-5
HARDCOVER ISBN: 978-1-5326-8232-2
EBOOK ISBN: 978-1-5326-8233-9

Manufactured in the U.S.A.   MAY 30, 2019

For Mary

Believing is seeing.

Contents

III. / 59

Acknowledgments

I AM GRATEFUL TO the editors of the following publications, in which some of these poems (a few with changes) first appeared:

5–2 Crime Quarterly: Sermon Notes

CCTE Studies: Logbook, Berth, Meditation on a Theme from Heraclitus, Picnic Near a Winter Wheat Field, Older Couple, Living in East Texas, Waiting for Another Sunset, Rain Walk, After an Ice Storm, Google Me, Advice to Someone Like Me, Waiting for Amnesia, Lines for Breakfast, Manuscripts in Hell

Concho River Review: Grandfathers, 1970

Furnace Review: Interglacial

Kind of a Hurricane Press (Tic Toc): Ambitions, Envelope

Lumina: Rereading Old Books, Talking to Myself on my Fortieth Birthday

Penwood Review: Church Picnic, Another Statement on Babel

St. Katherine Review: Monster Minds

Southwestern American Literature: Meditation in the Texas Hill Country, Lost Prerogative, Felling Bois D'Arc

Triggerfish Critical Review: Subterranean Music, Looking for Fossils in the Sulphur River

I.

Meditation in Texas Hill Country

Whatever this countryside is, it's not
art for art's sake. Rises buckle
who knows how from sea floors
we call prehistoric because we
weren't standing here taking notes.

Crushed shell and coral transformed,
now shed limestone talus and scrabble
in late spring sunlight, a still life
of disintegration, a story set in naked
sediment and eroding fault lines.

Scrub oaks borrow height from hills
along aquifer-fed springs which activate
molecular machinery of prickly pear,
oleander, and spiny lizards down at life's
basement level in the mist of quarks and gluons.

Placed in adjectival region between vast and slight,
we can't guess the architect's meaning behind
this dogged impermanence and temporary solidity.
Lighter than the dust blown down slope into our eyes,
we know only the heft of the sky's larger frame.

Ambitions

When I was ten, stars played at evading
the clutch and swing of backyard oak trees
and hid in my finger span. I thought I'd
join their game, but math dunked my mind
into magnitude, and constellations
fled to the far end of my telescope.

At fifteen, I longed to dig the next Troy
but found I'd be mining through the slag
of years melted under mindless sun's heel,
imperfectly resurrecting potsherds
into heavens of study and disuse
like all the mis-glued models on my shelves.

Twenty's ideal saw me a nomadic
forest ranger, guarding wetlands or perched
on watch towers staring down smoke signals,
but cigarette butts and burned pines
made me want to feed bears junk-food
tourists or to bank their cameras in leaves.

Now I teach texts to forests of students.
Some eat snacks while touring cell phones,
but others bring me splintered sentences,
shards strained from sediments of their pasts.
I patch and mend until stars breeze overhead,
configuring glory in skies beyond our kin.

Looking for Fossils
in the Sulphur River

Hoarded now in a tea tin on my writing desk,
relics rattle when shaken, surviving memory's
blank weather, fragments carelessly denoting
unbroken story lines scarcely extant in mind.

I crawled for hours in channels of deep time,
my sixth-grade mind focused on finger-sieving
the piebald gravel, screening chunks of monster
mesosaurs, sharks, and stony, wrinkled worms.

Their moment had passed, bones and teeth turned
to stone, gnashed and buried by water and time,
reappearing like textbook's faulty memory
of an ancient king's abdicated scepter and crown.

Still protruding from its piece of flinty gum,
a shark's tooth rests in my palm; just longer
than the first two joints on my index finger,
it narrows to a point that could still wound.

Grandfathers, 1970

Uncentered, my grandfathers loiter
by Florida orange trees blurred by wind
beyond the narrow camera's view.
As if knowing they would not see
the new decade's finish, neither smiles.
No pictures record the rest of the day,
but I can guess what came next:
One drove home to his photography
and pacifism, traveling toward the day
he was attacked and killed
by his weak but kindly heart.
The other walked back into his watch shop
to work on gears and motors,
not seeing through his jeweler's glass
the night he would fall asleep
and slip into silence like a clock
someone forgot to wind.

Felling Bois d'Arc

Maybe in an untended angle of Eden
before we named bristle and barb,
their first seed swelled and set root.

God's curse made them modern
and they sprouted thorns, leaned down,
and began protecting their strange secrets.

They leak warm milk blood when cut.
Ripped yellow wood splinters upward,
biting back at chain saw blade.

Graceless, whether growing or dropping,
they clutch the trees around them,
rending forest shade as they fall.

Just as problematic prone as standing,
they pierce hands and feet, granting
hours of pain from heartwood's pure venom.

But they guard with pike and poison
only a crop mocking heavy grapefruit—
a kind of apple horses alone love.

The wood never rots; stumps uncovered
decades later could almost serve as anvils
on which to beat ploughshares into swords.

The Caddo's stone axes smoothed limber bows
from the yellow wood long before railroads
employed it for ties, pavement stones, and wheel stock.

Few craftsmen have the patience now to buff
limbs down to mellow finish or transform
the trees' stubbornness into table and chairs.

Now mainly fence posts along county roads,
they twist from the plumb of any honest standard,
and elbow barbed wire across Texas fields.

Plunked in postholes and tamped tight with dirt,
they resist termites and other entropies.
Rootless, they rise again.

Losing Bois d'Arc Creek

These woods hide houses and leaves,
shards of lives broken by time,
fused and annealed in memory's glare.

Dug in the corner of what was a yard,
lined with bricks burned in kilns far from here,
a circle engraves bottomland.

Like the bucket that once dipped the water table
from this dark hole, memory is too heavy to hold
at a spell's end frayed like rope.

Scan the volumes of fields and wood now,
for sketches of those who lived in green shadows,
before cities insist that water stand still just here

for their own reasons, wiping off lives
like mud from boots on a wooden porch
or fingerprints from a sweaty lemonade pitcher.

Once lives stretched out among these trees,
upholding recollection like clotheslines
where clean shirts and overalls taunted wind.

Small-spoken hunters and farmers, mouths
round with the accents of an almanac
speaking sun, moon, root and grain, must give way

before lawns where the guardians of green,
nitrogen and phosphorus, kill the unworthy
dandelions planting themselves like mule hooves.

How many times must the lives of the few
bow before the needs of the many and memory
snap before the weight of new lives?

"Always" says the augury of jet-ski wakes
carved from runoff that the kingdom-come
of driveways and street gutters now permits.

Day on Little Pigeon

The river counts slowly to one hundred,
then begins again, as you and I climb
to the back of a boulder some glacier
pinched off and lodged grave and snug
as a conductor before an orchestra.
The river reads signals for smooth legato,
disguising dissolution's omnipresence
and fraying its fingered strings over low falls.

We stretch prone across cool granite
to cup water and break stone-shaped
metrics that tally leaves barging
over a concentrated tempo of swells,
while twigs barque toward some
downstream coda of waterlog polish
and rot beyond light's measuring rods.

Running words can't capture this spree
of spray, shiver and unwilling travel.
Still, we might be going somewhere,
sprawling in winter sunshine's bare notice,
riding our rocky raft through rapid's abrasion
toward a quiet sediment of dark and rest.

Picnic near a Winter Wheat Field

Late afternoon, bread-full and feast-finished,
we stumbled through the day's story.

Bright air swallowed every other word while
grass armies with blades we couldn't tally

counted cadences below our notice,
marched to the tick of sunlight's metronome.

We rested for that moment in sense and nonsense,
cupping laughter, swigging silences,

unaware that we would learn each other
like the inflected language of a myth

that time turns true.

Red Oak Leaves, April Morning

Buoyant, they strain like hot-air
balloons tethered at a county fair.
Tree seems to grip earth, avoiding flight,
but the leaves act like it's only a matter of time

before they wrest trunk and roots dripping
dirt into sky. The wind drones,
"You'll soon be done," but leaves keep
ringing suns into year's circle.

Light trips over them, shattering cells,
turning their near-transparency brown
more slowly than seeing allows.
The leaves will settle somewhere

in the dictionary of all their days,
bookmarked between *depart* and *drift*,
but today they're perfectly undropped,
as if they didn't believe in October.

After Ten Years

Entering the pact,
speaking those words,
we did not know then
what we do not know now:
how it will end, or when.
All we know is nothing
separates us from God's love—
a death we hang onto for dear life.
Meanwhile, we wait for the answers
to arrive after we finish our riddles.
Watching through these days,
we have withstood time's cadence
filled and empty, wind and water.
Love, more is still to come—this working,
this waiting that is ours, together.

Morning Spider

She hangs like a drop of brimstone,
a widowed queen who might whisper
"The king is dead, long live the queen."
Her legs dip night from heavens
she holds at bay, and her body's
all golden fruit draped on a black tree.

Writing from her inner voice,
she twists her radial grammar
tight against Spring's loose diction,
and her bite punctuates sleep's sentence
with a final full stop: Providence.

She sips a dozen blades of garden green
from a hopper with sky-blue eyes
that laughing children, always learning,
have tossed into this morning's mesh.

Google Me

Like columns of army ants
cutting a rain forest at night,
my names march past.
Not doppelgangers, but ghosts
I ping with no self-echo:

Little league umpire, conflict resolver,
dragster builder, photographer, librarian,
musician, firefighter, businessman,
janitor, inventor, criminal,
author, tenor, painter, pallbearer

They breathe in cities I've never known,
find friends I've never made, fasten
to me only by name's accident.
Yet all my desires branch choice's tree,
root earth center, plunge deepest sky.

Hinges of Hell

August in Texas and, castor smooth,
Satan's throne rolls closer by the hour.
The sky swipes its tongue across wincing fields,
and stones store up heat for judgment day.
Intent on no evil near this horizon, clouds
ford pools of super-heated air on sunlight stilts,
migrating to some Canaan beyond our borders.

Even now, living through this purgatory,
salted with fire, we know that any future
sky-kindness will likely be the killing kind.
Tongues of fire will veer to volleys of rain,
and small towns and trailer-parks known only
from weather reports will sight twisters, dodge
golf-ball hail and buckle under straight-line winds.

Today, though, halos of heat's holocaust twist
barbs into our brows. We wait fall's resurrection.

Stories I Tell Myself

Some nights, voices din worlds
into my brain's furrows
like loose marbles on a Chinese checker board.
I hush their clatter with an amulet,
perhaps a word like *avalanche,*
and bury myself in a small cabin
hanging on cliff's edge—
basalt, untouched by pitons or rope.
Lantern, candle, even match, all gone,
and no one to find the tin holding an intricate map
with the secret of hidden gold.
Dark suspends sound in a simple syrup
of low frequency as bats swim
through spheres of dark echo,
and I sleep sheer, dreamless myth.

Midnight Pantoum, Galveston Beach

The ocean's a factory that grinds the shoreline.
Tonight, white-edged gears and conveyors
rip the marrow from beach's bones.
Deep water can make us disregard our destiny.

Tonight, white-edged gears and conveyors
lift freighter's cargo and knead stone to silt.
Deep water can make us disregard our destiny;
imagine a pebble unmoved by ocean's will.

Lift freighter's cargo and knead stone to silt;
from this broth, moon-seasoned dunes will rise.
Imagine a pebble unmoved by ocean's will,
composing music under a still sky.

From this broth, moon-seasoned dunes will rise;
rip the marrow from beach's bones.
Composing music under a still sky,
the ocean's a factory that grinds the shoreline.

Dreams, Then Waking

I swim a long-winded river
under a spiral of hawking dragonflies,
or thresh rye with the blades
of quarter horse hooves.
The biased sun reels
memory's threads like an angler
with an empty hook.

Metaphors melt in the end
of morning's glassworks,
let fall messages of clear nothing
that last through night's distance.
Lost in symbol's hazard,
my mind swerves past unfallen worlds,
and my hands reach for Eden's neck.

Lines for Breakfast

This morning, I'm not hiking the continental divide
nor soaring over high-pressure ridges in my mind;
I'm just trying to heave myself over the high fence
of me and mine sometime before lunch.

Here, on the fading waxed table top,
I trace chewed index nail through self's finish,
sketching the outline of future days
I lack the faith to believe won't include me.

Meanwhile, Sun, that central character
in our daily myths, hints nothing of what's to follow—
the day's map is soggy with disinformation
like cereal left to milk's devices.

The particular plain, valley, or ridge,
past which nerves grant only ghosts,
lies hidden in swirls of invisible contour lines,
like fingerprints time will leave on tomorrow's knife.

Sun Room, October Morning

I sit here this morning like a drunken weaver,
mistaking the simplest points of weft and warp.
Looming overhead, sky giants twist and dye
oak leaves into the splurge of season's finish,
click cold limbs with doom's tapered needles.

I may chatter and fray through words' blanket,
but I'm still unwearied by the bight of sunrise
and sparrows, bacon and eggs, plaited together
in this corner where, for now, only a few dead
leaves slip-stitch a worn-out spider's web.

Rereading Old Books

Before you unlock your old books and discover
marginalia, long forgotten but not quite illegible,
written in a hand sharing your fingerprints,
mull over the hazards of yesterday's faded timbre.
You ride a raft of paper to make night landfall
on a continent, where beaches give way to jungles.
The few clearings might reveal ruins of people
whose dialect runs like groundwater down steps
leading to a cenote, falls into flooded caves
to the feet of a rain god grumbling to himself.
Here is no altar, no stone knife, no ripped heart raised
to the sun—only shadows painted before you arrived.

Were you hoping for something else?

When you shove aside the tangled liana and creeper,
you may well lay bare a Rosetta Stone of unfaded inscriptions
whose tongues chant stars steering in lost configurations,
but the gloss you recover may also crack the covert
semaphores you have used once too often.

Preparing for Winter

Time still might remain to finish our stories
before cold's vacant presence saps these fields,
setting seeds to dream their furious green lives.
Clouds promise futures we might misconstrue.

Before cold's vacant presence saps these fields,
can we hope that sorrow, too, obeys seasons?
Clouds promise futures we might misconstrue,
and wind gossips stories we shouldn't trust.

Can we hope that sorrow, too, obeys seasons?
The sky's tarnished compass drives us in circles,
and wind gossips stories we shouldn't trust
just before winter's vacuum tubes begin to hum.

The sky's tarnished compass drives us in circles,
and late summer seems relieved to renounce its light.
Just before winter's vacuum tubes begin to hum,
time still might remain to finish our stories.

Talking to Myself
on My Fortieth Birthday

Think of a horse clicking over brick roads
in a winter measured by sundials.

Don't think about each day's museum
where you've left dust-bound footprints.

Assume sand pinches though hourglasses,
springs stretch hands across taut clock faces.

Don't assume the stars' careful count has kept track
of all the hours and days you've misplaced.

Remember foam turning rocks under waterfalls,
blackbirds straining across the sky's skein net.

Forget last spring's final leaf caught briefly
in your coat collar on its flight from air to mold.

Consider your mind complete in middle night;
be unwoven by morning's partial sentence.

Close your eyes; all the world pours down the throats
of hummingbirds whose first songs you've lost.

Interglacial

Pushing down the permanent snow line,
cold snouts of glaciers shoved forests flat,
heaved earth and trimmed rock over grasslands,
mounted moraines over murdered dominions.

You and I were born in a flash off winter's mirror,
a single sweat drop of time. Safe in our
temperate spell, we deny the rimed flume's return,
the bitter flow bearing a slow, single measure.

Frosty eons will lid green nature's x'd eyes
as Earth rolls on arctic bed, snugging up ice sheets
and coiling fervid dreams, plotting an age without us.
For now, we restrain blizzards of blank space.

Intertwined, our thermal columns rise,
aloof to smoking cold air and all icy threats
of solar withdrawal. Flesh ablaze in our cirque,
we live in this molten moment where Earth,
at its roiling iron core, knows no seasons.

II.

Another Statement on Babel

Yes, we built a city with a tower
far away from untrustworthy oceans.
Our bodies had ached from long-winded years
spent skirmishing the friendless earth.

It's true; we refused to fill the world with
our wandering any longer. Granted,
we wanted a name and maybe some path
away from the dust we were becoming,

away from the creator's dark genius
that slimed our drinking water, slithered through
our grain fields, and hunted us when we left
our caves to burn our dead like old cordwood.

In the beginning, laughter and backslapped
congratulations were the day's language.
But soon the bulk of muttered curses massed,
nudging wheelbarrows up the corkscrew ramp.

I remember clearly: construction cost
over-runs, labor disputes, the fluent
disagreements among our architects;
trust me, God had nothing to fear from us.

We baked bricks, stacking, and tarring;
our scaffolded turrets needled the sky.
Work days closed, and the heavens felt closer,
but every morning, they floated Eden-far.

Then came the day we gained God's attention,
and he spilled us like ants from a
heel-flattened hill. Our ears began to throb
with the clank and thud of new accents.

We listened for matching voices, but heard
no harmony, only rubble of glides and
trampled fricatives. I clenched a trowel,
hunting a name I'd used the day before,

but old words faded even as I thought them.
Standing still as sandstone in tower's shadow,
ignoring the gibberish of the rabble,
I grouped and counted my family.

We clung together trying not to speak, ears
covered against gutturals, chirps, and grunts—
vowels without weight or measure, syllables
snarled and crashing like fractured keystones.

We scratched stick figures in the sand,
to cry "I still love you," "Don't leave."
"I want to stay together." We finally packed,
gathered our dogs, and wandered away.

No map ever returns us to the site,
but our dreams assemble stones despite all
conviction. Many nights, sculpted walls sing
in chorus of height with no fear of fall,

no whiff of sweaty arms or trace of tar.
Joist, purlin, and truss raise a helix to
the surrounding sky, where frictionless clouds
skim past windows without drops of judgment.

Beneath high-pitched roof of water and wind,
I overhear supple, splashing speech,
puffs of laughter, potent prose spraying in
cooling shades of nuance and allusion,

dialect needing no translator or gloss.
All lips speak an unwritten language sealed
within covers of a final concordance.
I wake with split tongue cemented in my mouth.

Monster Minds

"...the earth sustains on her bosom many monster minds—minds which are not afraid to employ the seeds of Deity deposited in human nature as a means of suppressing the name of God."

—John Calvin

Maybe I'm that mind,
an astronomer hoisting data
like a fish testing water mass
with cataract's plummet.
I strain numbers none have read,
declare disaster for dead galaxies,
then fall asleep to the garble
of background radiation
battering through time.
Morning will see me trampling
fall's Pentecost of leaves,
prying into heavens emptied
of all but bare branches
and crossed only by cumulus.

Or maybe you're that mind,
a naturalist, muttering
"*felis catus*," over tiger tracks
near a creek bed where
crayfish molt under leaf rot,
and honey bees sip in the shallows,
balanced on water's moment
like waiters' wine carafes—

all items in your research log,
except for the stone rolled
across your path: nothing
but erosion chewing granite resistance.
You return samples to the lab
to spend years, analyzing.

Subterranean Music

Till today, I expected your life to emerge
from the rocks near where I last saw it sink,
to flow lucid into daylight once more.
Our last talk tottered on brittle laughter;
major intervals lowered half a step to minor notes.

Like a spelunker who leaves sun-lit surfaces
and drops into caverns of stalagmite groves,
you descended, pitching your bass clef by dark pools,
corpse-pale, composing some somber continuo
of stars bound in skies you couldn't trust to hold them.

Persuaded by gentle fingers and palms, felt-covered
hammers strike steel strings, energy and air bond,
resonating with all the placid grace of your angry mind:
Those thoughtful songs, designed to escape thought,
performed in private or in lashing sheets of applause.

Your life's clear, untroubled brook mists away
into mere invention; my ear missed some modulation,
some tone beyond my range while you meditated.
Tunneling despair, phosphorescent with mimetic joy,
you surfaced in a Sahara, lapped up by summer's tongue.

Logbook

Your mind crashes
into this cold day
like an icebreaker
in the north Atlantic
searching sullen pack ice.
You drive over
crusted coffee cups
that blend dead leaves
with yellow warning paint
peeled from the curb
of an auto parts store.
Power poles and auto fenders
pinch your brain's prow
but mark your position
in a changing instant,
sketch an impersonal cipher
of events that unfold
like sheets of an aurora.
Your destination lacks
mathematical certainty,
but pressure behind
and before hints
any stop along this day
might jam you like
an arctic floe beneath a sky
the sun will soon forsake.

The Seafarer: A Late Interpolation

I'm writing no apology, but mark
my words; using demolition's dialect,
I've served like a deckhand on a destroyer,
rolling nouns and verbs like depth charges,
delighting in floating wreckage, oil slicks,
and all the sobbing air bubbles
that sign love's last-known location.
I've cut language loose, leaving it
to float unattached like the ghost nets
of trawlers long ago returned to port.
Snares continue to haunt quiet bays
where our love-winded spinnakers
once romped, and the sun's blinding zero
subtracted all our days' score.
I stretch now over warped planks
and slap my speech into wave after wave
I hope will reach where you vanished,
wordless, in the slam of anger's wake.

Hard of Hearing

I don't know what I don't know
and my mind can't slip
like a merchant ship under
your Gibraltar guns,
to unload cargo you won't sign for.

Your squall line has slapped me
toward a down measured in miles
sunk from sun's sight to broken rest
on mounds beneath dust's rain
that sludges ocean floor.

I know my mind's sickness
can't be cured by ownership alone,
nor by simply renouncing my hold
on everything. All I've missed
is a megaphone you press to my ear.

Morning, Noon, and Night

The sorrowful serpent
hums in your ears,
packing your head with pitch—
tales true or not,
best ignored either way.
Still, you hound your doom
down its daily rat hole,
twisting like entrails
from a slaughtered ox.
Afterward, aimless
as a September wind, silence
shreds the season to incense,
unburned in a dark church.

Haunts

I thought some editor had finally silenced them
like spare cats dunked in a murky roadside creek,
return envelope sack-smothering final heartbeats.

But some dark nights, I'll hear one keening over
injustice and lack of love as its feet stutter down
the hallway past the bookshelves into my study.

Another peers over my shoulders as I write
and hisses death on the fresh page before me,
willing its corpse back into my corpus.

My fists tighten on their spines, but they escape
like blobs of mercury from a broken barometer
through cracks under my desk, return to their dark nidus,
scratching for attention when they think I'm alone.

Manuscripts in Hell

Deep in hell's bowels,
old-fashioned printing presses
grind out the gruel of confession,
while Satan and all his bards
scratch their scabs and write
close observations of nature,
or nature and death,
or love, death, and nature
or the nature of dead love:
words, words, words.
They're piled to the cavern roof
even with constant ignition.
Forever tone deaf
and quite unrepentant,
undead poets snake out sonnets
and sestinas without end,
while their brethren
the novelists claw for characters
no one will care for
enough to kill.

Yet Another Ars Poetica

Words should not strangle winter
moonlight in tree branches they recall,

nor be merely magnets to draw us back
to sanity after daylight's petty thieveries.

They might lug the fruit of argument
like a wheelbarrow with a low tire,

but hear them grind a lens to magnify
mountains or shrink body to cell.

Words might not tell you how to feel
about mica flashing suns off a mesa,

nor about your father's face ghosting
a window of your middle-aged house,

but watch them locate crayfish groping prey
in caves under Kentucky fields,

or smear your eyes till the world's a smoke
of cinnamon and hail-shot on tin roof.

Poetry can't replace hatred or love,
but it might breach your bedroom at midnight

and whisper its blade across your throat,
waking you to grope for stars just past your ceiling.

Reading an Old Novel
during a Thunderstorm

With broken tongues dragged through the dust
of our dead-beat world, we pose our riddles
and worry the blueprints of archetypes,
while sharing space with lava flow,
Richter scale, and hooks on Doppler radar.
Meanwhile, rusty nails shrill out
from the warped boards falling
from this dead barn lying in
an old defeat of sun and rain.

God the Magician

Swaddled and safe in our padded pews,
we hail God like he's a dated headliner
on a Vegas stage, a conjurer sandwiched
between improv acts and our late lunch.

Yarns of grace befuddle us as we hang
in the harness of our long yawns.
We ponder men hacked in half but
offered whole later in the program

and suppose straightforward solutions:
hidden wires, false panels, hinged boxes,
but he yanks bloody scarves from his sleeves
and wooden men vault to life and sing.

We call them ventriloquist dummies,
believing also that the dozens of doves
from his top hat burst from cages below stage,
our faith suspended in solutions of ease.

Eyes misdirected, we stray through riddles
of motion and sleight but fail to track his hands
unweaving time with slow signature shifts,
breaking the lonely liturgies of ordinary life.

We stand to leave, polite but hungry,
tramping like tourists toward buffets
we can believe in, hands hot for slot-machines
made for congregations of the numb.

Invisible again, God follows us, floating
above falling mountains of dust motes,
each strobing light whose source we've lost.

Sermon Notes

In a church with an atrium
like a Gulfstream hangar,
ushers herded their sheep
past coffee shop and bookstore,
comforting with blue-tooth staffs.

A stadium posed as sanctuary
with a pulpit like a mound
where the ace pitched a promise
to spot the best me: wanted,
and missing so long.

But the best me loitered
like a lookout man, chain-smoking
outside a mid-western bank:
banshee tires, gunfire,
another town.

All My Small Designs

Against the taut circles of time's pulse
I lay my cheek, checking on parts of my story,
seeking some slight trace of gold in streams
dried dead long since, or running somewhere
else beyond all hope or guess.

Damned spring serpent—you who slammed the door
and wiped your feet on minds smaller than yours—
you keep cracking tales of ruin and spoil.
What person has not felt the old smash
of time's hail, the wave of withering?

Outside ancient garden, against briar and rose
I ail, unable to break gates or climb walls
disguised as one no swords seek.
Restrained light surrounds me, revealing
old scars I would paint with smiles if I could.

Forests fall, rot and vanish, then rise again.
I can't pioneer a way out of history.
Cut from the firm shape of the former world,
memory's planks slam along in dark brain tide,
rebuffing sunlight's pure intention.

Every way in only leads further out
to a place of skulls I deny every day.
Mind's margins, demarked spaces I re-cross,
the fields of all my small designs shine
like polar ice too cold for winter wandering.

Elijah, after Ravens

I felt like a cliff face, cracked
by runoff after rain as God
poured his message down
in fragments I still can't decipher.

The ravens' wings masked intention.
I never touched them, though I tried;
they crammed morsels of carcass
into my mouth like I was their hatchling.

Their presence mystifies me less now
that they are absent. I see no black
points in the wind, nor imagine
their return any time soon.

I have prayed and fasted here
until prosperity's stream dried.
My tongue is an etched tablet I share
with none as I chew my prayers.

Peak and Trough

Peak chuckles at Trough's expense—
misunderstands his obsession with knives and guns,
grasps nothing of rage,
reckless endangerment of permanent peace.

Trough hunkers in his tower where light is taboo,
gnaws bones fallen from his company of corpses.
He guards unlighted torch and caldrons of oil,
ready to pour hell on peace's siege in an instant.

Peak sees clouds sailing unhindered
by graver thoughts of earth, releases weight
when skies begin to darken,
strokes hackles of occasional fears back to calm.

Trough glares at Peak, wonders why
illusion rewards such stupidity with content,
scrapes his close-chewed nails across the chalkboard
of his face, lips parting only to hiss at the silence.

Peak wishes that Trough would stop scowling at him
in the mirror as day jockeys to pass day.
Trough wishes he could get his claws around
Peak's throat and teach him to cry for mercy.

Lament and Reply

I.

I'm sick of gnawing my heart
over the flesh that falls from bone,
tired of groping in future's empty sack
for today's bread and cheese.
Sorrow falls in lines and curves
I can't cipher without an algorithm
dropped from my DNA.
I can't bear season's pilfering:
All I thought was arctic now melts,
cathedrals, oak trees, old ideas—
change just masks trickster *loss*.

II.

You are not a rock,
resting in stream bed yet.
Rushing days may leave you aloof,
but today can skip like a stone
across your sorrow's surface tension.
Old notions may evaporate and reform.
Make way for glacier's resurrection
to grind down crags of hopelessness.
Wait for the word to unbolt the night.
Pay no heed to all you've lost;
time thieves only your pocket change.

Waiting for Amnesia

The mind washes
away memory, blusters

cobwebs. In spiders
the shadows of self,

or a ghost. What
steals doubt but certainty

of failure, and who
attends funerals

before the moon ends
toiling tides

and drowning? Under
breakers of wakefulness,

repose. Beaches grow
nothing but alpha waves

of winter wheat. Cows
crop heavy

plenty: green tang
and total desire.

What chain links hand
staff and helve?

Rain. Cornfields planed
flat to horizon.

Crows drop knives
on deserts built

beneath cities. Lobes
of time settle

for less and less,
hoard damage and loss.

Recall, nothing
but sinkholes in freeways.

Down swallows dawn; dark
rubs out day;

shades settle to silt. Forget
the sea.

Rain Walk

Water beats like bare feet cordial with concrete.
Our yews pelt me with invisible drops
as I brush their poison, tonight, just past
the front door that I shut behind me as I walk out.

The rain falls without memory of having fallen before;
already, it forgets clouds, sky, itself.

Only lakes and rivers, so small under foot,
remember and store the past for future use
on a day we can't imagine, after the sun surrenders
and night again pushes its dark cargo down our street.

Advice to Someone Like Me

Write so slowly you change by sentence end.
Your exile to another plane of existence waits,
so savor slipstream moments, tugging you
toward different locations and contexts.
Script future roles for your dead-weight selves.
Perhaps you'll roll like a dolphin in some fabled sea,
or drop like a sinker dragging shark bait:

You will know when you get there,
if *there* remains a place when you arrive,
after that slow sculptor, earth,
presses your brow under his thumbs,
finding the contours that clarify
character's intent before your features
melt into the mush of time's marsh.

What am I talking about?
How many metaphors will you need
before you understand?
Metaphors satisfy only the mind,
and the mind satisfies only itself,
leaving little space for the heart
to labor over its tiny puzzles
in the darkness and quiet of your chest.

Inner Ring

Like hedges around an exclusive club,
a trimmed-mean circle allows the select
to chat and sport in friendship's flame.
Outside, just our binary communion.

Beyond their walled courtyards
that guard inside jokes and gossip,
let us pronounce benediction and then
savor some small benefit of the fringe.

Past oaks blocking halogen's glare,
our gaze may adjust to darkness,
gauging the stars swept into patterns
shaped to suit us in solitude's slack outliers.

After an Ice Storm

Above the fields' cold furnace,
clearing sky tends increments of ice.
Branches sag like standards
from a battle already decided.

Shrugging elms surrender worlds
of water clutched from frozen night,
but not before winter's knife has slashed
their symmetry to stump and stub.

More random than rain, thaw
drips fluid keys of enigma code,
and light buffs beads falling
back into bedlam's hoard.

Overhead, confetti cirrus scrawls
remnants of dot and dash,
traces our broken lines
and myths of power, again.

Lost Prerogative

After fall, vision falters, but still the red-tail's
white underwings trace the sky like a stylus.
Sharp-eyed, he scribes letters in quick language
untranslatable into our race's worn tongue.

I lounge on my back in the dust and tired broom sage,
trying to decode this circumsolar calligraphy.
Rummaging my dialect, I hunt the proper spell
to bend his spirals down to my shoulder, unable
to find a voice to circumscribe such wide autonomy.

Hawk ends letter with relaxed gesture, sealing
the blue like an imperial signet pressing melted wax.
Dropping through provinces of cool air, he delivers
his message to a corn snake hunting rats of this realm.

Viva

I've wandered like some stranded traveler
stumbling through an unnamed desert,
eyes tied to one mirage after another,
water holes yanked from blind day.

I've carried your words under my tongue,
rolling their pebble smoothness
under the roof of my mouth,
wringing life from hard stone.

I savor what I can't understand·
grace asked over the last lamb
in a feast for a prodigal returning to life
from a far country.

After Twenty Years

Morning, and affection arrives
like the summer mail, all warm-
colored ads and mute invoices
we toss on the kitchen table.

All afternoon, love writhes and fumes
like heat from an underground forge,
hammer on anvil, steel smoke,
temper annealed to stroke and shock.

Evening consummates time's flux,
and we forget our faces and the names
of stars that smolder into the sky
like welding arcs seen from a safe distance.

Night keens the kinetics of decay,
half-life shimmer and flare, but still here
and there, still you and I, bonded elements,
dissolve together toward sunrise.

III.

Berth

Roving around the stone slabs
your calendar chips into months,
you could be tempted to despair
if you considered only a chart chronicling
longitudes of despair and latitudes of hope.

Though unheralded by full moon or holy day,
this moment offers a berth, snug as a liner's cabin,
with only the sun prodding through a porthole
to check your presence, to see if you're paying attention,
still, to each wave that lifts and drops you
into tomorrow and tomorrow and tomorrow.

Waking before Alarm Clock

Waiting for the old magic to flow
from my life's secret conduits,
I lie like an egg, still and unscrambled
before the demands of day's deal cutting.

I keep each care-filled breath separate
from my hope for quotidian miracles
of sunlight and shadow, leaf fall and root growth.
Still, I can't buy a dream on morning's open market.

Custom deadens fresh seeing, yet
the familiar light touching the tops of the oaks
might still transmute this new day
from leaden slugs to golden hoard

on which dragons lounge and yawn,
waiting to fly against today's stark patent,
breaking my cold fast with credulity
and reshaping the self I lost in the night.

New Year's Day

One day, and time bounds
somehow in a new track,
not with the distinction
minted in snowflakes,
but in ordinary grass and stone,
frozen in present affliction,
but drifting toward a July
jelled deep in our pockets.
Winter will empty like a balloon
and stir us toward hours
bearing the white marks of joy,
binding us with contentment's chords.

General Revelation

Lancing from red leaves
twisted on fall's gallows,
the common tongue
pours out a daily idiom.

Love's sweet stammer
reaches the easy dialect

of quiet Tuesday evenings
when children sleep,
keeps time polishing dishes
and picking up cracker crumbs,

whispers grace over all
we can't know yet,

cascades over eyelids
blinked shut against
winter sun's riddles—
warmth, brightness, certainty.

God the Alchemist

Leaning about God's lawn,
our bodies wait, ruined statues—
scrap, subject to heavy melting.

We cannot turn our trove of lead
to treasure, cannot distill magic,
base metal's universal solvent.

We harrow poison over golden fields,
beyond all hope after autumn's dirge.
Dust can only reimburse dust.

But God, standing before his eternal retort,
crystalizes our new nature from elements
not found on the periodic chart, speaks

a secret name into nothing
and lights the candle of new creation.

Church Picnic

Held down by bowls of mustard potato salad,
pan-fried chicken breasts, five-cheese pasta,
and a shallow dish of mysterious pickles,
the shroud of tablecloth retorts the wind's flail.

Laughter runs around me in spirals
of small children and charcoal smoke.
Sparrows fall from trees, wronging gravity
at the last second, questing crumbs.

Misplaced salad tongs prod through
chicken parts. Green olives roll away,
and waiting earth begins to weave
dropped deviled eggs into ant's architecture.

Dripping planks of pork ribs invite me
to platter flood and char in balanced portion.
I wrestle with uncut sourdough, loafing
in its plastic-wrap like Lazarus in grave clothes.

An old man in the line across from me laughs
and shouts "Come out!" freeing the bread
and tearing a hunk for my bowed paper plate.
The wind baffles me with joy's persistence.

John VI, 53 ff

This flesh tenders conflict,
wrapped raw around mystery,
a wineskin brimming blood birth,
a still life hung in time's flume.

Wrapped raw around mystery,
grace slakes the lonely with presence,
a still life hung in time's flume.
Eating death, we follow life in forfeit.

Grace slakes the lonely with presence;
though days wrench and crush,
eating death, we follow life in forfeit,
multiplying even as we divide.

Though days wrench and crush,
together, we confess our famine.
Multiplying even as we divide,
joy swirls past our broken tongues.

Meditation on a Theme from Heraclitus

"There await men when they die such things as they look not for nor dream of."

Some lives long to close but fail
to notice how final quiet catches them,
sinking to sleep on the lap
of a spell they've long awaited.

Intoned to peace by season's schedule,
they don't feel the hand that closes their eyelids
like a wind that seals the earth after rain's benediction,
crossing ground where forest once flourished.

Hearts, wills, and memories may miscarry,
but bounded chaos will slowly amend all they've left,
the ripped bags of good and bad, failure and success,
names, places, guilt, and good intentions.

Like wanderers whose home countries
long ago cast them out, they've finally been found
on a road leading toward a tomorrow they can't imagine—
an unsought land under a new sun not of their own devising.

Homily on Sorrow and Joy

Careening after consolations made extinct in another age,
we all strive through our own landscapes' still forms.
Ever-changing wind strobes around heads and torsos
of statues into which we pour our liquid lives.

Hospitals, churches, and cemeteries rest in easy proximity
along roads where the prodigal spirit of the age
chases its obscure ends, spending golden pennies
from its almost bottomless hoard, investing here, endowing there.

So tempting, to craft air's ever-present soul into grief—
a metaphor so apt because of its quiet refusal to close
its own books and stop reading aloud to rapt audiences
that always nod off before story's end.

But similes of joy, too, must have their say, like God's breathing
that smooths new flesh from old scars and replaces carrion
with grass and trees, locating delight within a few minor characters
in time to foreshadow happy endings over season's horizon.

We could hold our hands over our ears and refuse to listen,
but the quiet darkness cannot keep out the helix
of breeze and storm, cannot coil away the mixed intentions
that escape even the principalities, past our nerves' highest reach.

Silver Anniversary

A fishhook sliver of fresh moon
still minds our mutual life's memories—
unfocused dreams angling along
beaches of a lake larger than our vision.

Awash in calendar's wake but
meshed in slender lines of joy,
we've known sun's sly-cast lures,
and night's nets of shadow and shock.

After all forecasts and through all weathers,
we've rested under the mantle of a providence
unhurried as harvest moons, holding true
even when floats and sinkers of cloud intrude.

Though blessings sometimes flay patience,
and peace may swivel to reeling dread,
love keeps catching us with its tangled tackle,
grace hangs on with no hazard of release.

Envelope

I'm sealing an envelope
to open next year
or maybe the year after—
confirming some benefits of air
today allots us, our portion
of smoke from a chimney
that stands over oak fire,
a whiff of wheat's gold,
transmuted to bread,
a memory of rain on the
Japanese yews after a night
of thunder dropped on our heads.
Wait, from under the door,
a whisper will announce today's
arrival, pressed into our hearts with
time's invisible signet ring.

Down the Guadalupe

Testing echoes in this minor canyon,
we glide inner tubes over gravel
bars and water-sliced slabs.
Gravity tends its more solemn affair,
kneading water against limestone bed,
sweeping dolomite, marl, and shale along
camber and curve, ever recommencing
infinity's symbol around cypress roots
and banks breasted with sleepy desire.
Our fingers follow the swirl of water's will
glancing over each other, sky, or water.
Later, grounding on some unnamed loop
long before the river stops, we'll relocate
the intentions we let drift this afternoon.
Releasing indifference, we'll sculpt our path
once more, just as the nimble moon begins to roll
and resound longing's roundabout course.

Nothing for Now

Remember your old dream?
After five decades, night-construed mirage
still spots you hovering on wind stream,
melding color palate of rock face and river bed.

In the lens of dream memory,
you are nimble light, tree darting,
floating through boulders' nest near cliff edge.
Words don't happen to trouble you.

You partake of no past nor future—
the sun merely buffs bottomless brink
and wind tide twists you timeless,
subtracting all logic and desire.

But today, wakeful under sun's knowing stare,
you see the lone leaf at the top of a red oak
and can't quite imagine the calling that carried it
from soil to summit—brief, so brief.

The waking ground sucks at your legs,
and you can't explain your own crawl;
you only know earth is patient,
calling all back to itself after a season.

Even mountains feel the year's plow,
lapsing into valleys and deserts.
Your heart, too, once lifted and light,
freights decay's frightfulness.

While you kneel, waiting for season's turn,
recall the light, the cliff, the depth; believe
vast future waits with freedom to cheat
the ten-thousand gravities of this grave world.

Older Couple, Living in East Texas

I might have written long ago, only imagining
an older couple, alive in small-town Texas,
puttering away on some quiet corner lot
over St. Augustine and Big Boy tomatoes,
summer squash and early frost, watching
grown offspring further fixing the family line.

Maybe I delayed because *older* kept funneling
away from me like dead star light from another galaxy
as I trafficked in career, marriage, and family
or watched friends caper among diapers and dogs.
Moonlight and sunshine kept making assumptions
I wasn't ready to relegate to line and break.

But now, the guitar I never learned to play
sits in a dark corner of our bedroom
under a gentle coat of dust, next to the antique
wardrobe with the broken catch, each fretting
in its own way stories of time spent elsewhere,
forgotten distractions that left only broken intent.

Teens slam through doors opening
on fall and summer, winter and spring.
Days and weeks begin to evade us,
though our weedy backyard garden still rises and falls
yearly, like a nagging pop song, sobbing
from a decade historians already stake out.

Books on subjects that moved us to tears, once,
now make us blink through our bi-focals,
as we recall nostalgia from a time before our bodies
reminded us of dust, or friends burned their hearts to ash,
before we realized that the cratered moon of our lives
has already passed middle night and rounds toward dawn.

Awaiting Another Sunset

It's never too early to consider nightfall;
evening, after all, might pour its amber ale
upon our heads sooner than we expect.

Who defeats entropy, even in limited terms?
Someone should at least pick up the leaves
left over from morning wind's exuberance.

Why go grubbing day's moldering envelope?
Time has addressed it to someone else
who has moved from the neighborhood.

Does a blown dandelion ask questions of the wind?
The sun should warn lawns with their airs
of short-lived precision that it favors low upkeep.

It's never too late to repent of all our repenting,
even if we have stuck our fingers through
the spinning sprocket of God's grace once too often.

Talking to a Red-tailed Hawk
at Sunset

Flying from the sun into evening,
where does your eye not light?
Yet you know nothing more
than the tight turn of hunger's mandate.

Beneath time's spinning ruin you hang,
a quill that must cease someday.
But today, mortal failure does not touch you—
only wind and sudden earth.

You do not remember yourself
as you grasp the single sky,
untroubled by yesterday or tomorrow.
Beyond human catastrophe you slip

through moments with stony heart
unlearned in any pity or joy I read into the story.
You worship in your own way the vital purchase,
sky visiting earth, blood sacrifice, rising

with white under wings as you circle and lift
strains of glory be to Father, Son, and Holy Ghost:
as in the beginning, now, and ever shall be—
world without end, amen and amen.

www.ingramcontent.com/pod-product-compliance
Lightning Source LLC
LaVergne TN
LVHW021616080426
835510LV00019B/2604